Hi! I'm Meridee...
Welcome to the Meridee Winters Musical Universe!

In this book – one of many in orbit around here – you will meet Norman and join him on an epic note quest through the Megamusical Meteor Mazes.

You may have heard that every force has an opposing force. Creativity ~~is~~ supreme in this universe, but there ~~are~~ creative ~~work~~ just be ~~skills~~, b ~~the forc~~ ~~dom~~ and protect creativity. On your journey, you will train in different hand positions, ledger lines, intervals, mnemonic devices, and more. Practice hard enough, and the results might just be creatively… explosive.

Now, take a deep breath, pack your space snacks, and prepare to escape Planet Blah!

Meridee Winters™ NOTE QUEST TABLE OF CONTENTS

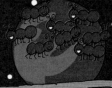

Meridee Winters Publishing • 63 W. Lancaster Ave. #7 • Ardmore, PA 19003
www.MerideeWintersMusicMethod.com
ISBN: 978-1-943821-57-0 • Library of Congress Catalog Control Number: 2018910340

Credits: Meridee Winters: Author, Creator, Art Director, Additional Illustrations
Kate Capps: Editor, Creative Consultant, Conceptual Conspirator • Krysta Bernhardt: Character Illustrations, Graphic Design
Sean Miller: Graphic Design, Illustrations • Armand Alidio: Cover/Graphic Design, Additional Illustrations • Monica Schaffer: Interval Innovator
Special thanks to Nicole Stranko and Gabriel Rhopers for Creative Consulting and Super Soundboarding during the design process.

SKILL DRILLS

SAY IT: As the teacher points to the notes, the student names them out loud

PLAY IT: As the teacher points to the notes, the student plays them on his/her instrument.

SAY IT AND PLAY IT: As the teacher points to the notes, the student plays and says the notes.

TIMED COMPETITION

How long does it take you to play the page? Time it and write it down on a score sheet. Can you beat your best time? Can you beat the other player's best time?

YOUR TIME: _____

★ BEST TIME: _____

MAZE

Each time you play, create a different pathway around the maze.

WAYS TO PLAY

STEADY BEAT CHALLENGE

Set the metronome. See if you can play/say all the notes at that speed. Each time you play, see if you can increase the tempo a bit. This is a performance/sight-reading skill.

TRACKING GAME

As the student plays/says one note, the teacher is already pointing to the next note to be played. Students can look ahead to prepare while playing/saying the current note. This works well in conjunction with the Steady Beat or Timed Competition games. This is a performance/sight-reading skill.

JELLY SWITCH

Switch! The student plays teacher and points to the notes while the teacher names or plays them! (Student favorite!)

NOTE HUNT GAME

The teacher plays a note on the keyboard. The student has to find all ocurrences of that note in the maze.

VARIATION: Piece Hunt! Pull out a piece of complicated music and do the note hunt game with that.

Join our community of teachers and curious creatives! Visit merideewintersmusicmethod.com

DON'T JOIN THEM

STAY BORING

3

JUST LIKE ALL CITIZENS OF PLANET BLAH, NORMAN WAS NORMAL. HE PLAYED PIANO USING THE SAME OLD BORING BOOKS, AND THEN HEADED OFF TO WORK AT THE BORING FACTORY.

BUT NORMAN WANTED MORE. HE'D HEARD OF AN ENTIRE MUSICAL UNIVERSE BEYOND PLANET BLAH, FULL OF CURIOUS CREATURES, FUN ADVENTURES, INTERESTING MUSIC AND... CREATIVITY.

IN A BOLD AND REMARKABLY UN-BORING ACT OF COURAGE, HE ESCAPED PLANET BLAH THROUGH THE BORING FACTORY'S FF EJECTOR (A WASTE EJECTOR FOR ANY TYPES OF FORBIDDEN FUN LIKE JOKES AND PICTURES).

NORMAN'S ADVENTURE HAD BEGUN! HE GAINED NEW MUSICAL POWERS AND MADE NEW FRIENDS.

MERIDEE WINTERS' MUSIC METHOD

NORMAN MAY HAVE ESCAPED PLANET BLAH, BUT HE SOON LEARNED THAT BORING FORCES WERE EVERYWHERE. THEY DREW HIM IN, BUT HE FOCUSED ON THE CREATIVE ENERGY INSIDE HIM...

AND HE WON! HIS CREATIVE POWERS TRIUMPHED OVER BOREDOM (IN A BATTLE SO EPIC THAT THE NOTES WERE FREED FROM THE STAFF TO START THEIR OWN ADVENTURES).

NORMAN'S QUEST FOR CREATIVITY BECAME PART OF MUSIC NOTE HISTORY... FOREVER KNOWN AS NOTE QUEST.

This book is dedicated to all of the dreamers out there who have the courage to learn something challenging in order to create something new.

IN AN ACTION-PACKED BLAST OFF, NORMAN ESCAPED HIS BORING MUSIC LESSONS ON PLANET BLAH. BUT HOW WOULD HE NAVIGATE THIS NEW UNKNOWN WORLD? HIS FIRST STEP TO UNLOCKING NEW MUSICAL POWERS WAS TO LEARN THE NAMES OF THE KEYS. SO HE HEADED TO THE PRE-READING GALAXY, ARMED WITH ONLY A FEW SPACE SNACKS (SOME FREEZE-DRIED BLAHBERRIES AND A TUBE OF IMITATION PEANUT BUTTER) AND A HUNGER FOR KNOWLEDGE. AND A HUNGER FOR REAL PEANUT BUTTER.

"Music is a universal language, and should be taught like one. But language isn't just about deciphering words — it's about having the tools to communicate your own ideas."

— *The Meridee Winters Guidebook to the Musical Universe*

TELESCOPIC TIPS:

Each of these versatile games can be played in a number of ways, from simply pointing and playing to navigating the pages like a board game. See page 3 for a list of ways to play.

For an entire galaxy of pre-reading music games that drill finger numbers, key names and rhythm, go to **merideewintersmusicmethod.com**

Close your eyes and put your finger on the page. Whatever letter you land on, find and play that note on your instrument. Can you play it in different octaves? (For an added challenge, use that note as the root of a chord, interval or scale. Pick several to create a chord progression or melody for a song.)

MERIDEE WINTERS®
MUSIC METHOD

Creativity Zone

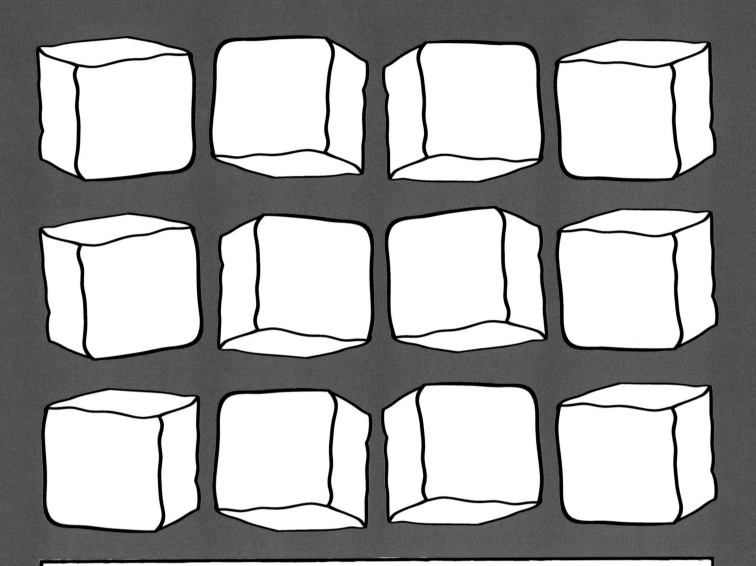

For a free printable download of this activity
and other fun stuff, visit **mwfunstuff.com/nqp**

CREATE
YOUR OWN
BLAST OFF
SCENE!

MERIDEE
WINTERS'
MUSIC METHOD

AFTER LEAVING THE PRE-READING GALAXY, NORMAN USED HIS NEW KNOWLEDGE OF NOTE NAMES TO NAVIGATE TO THE SPACE FACE METEOR SYSTEM. FROM THE FRIENDLY SPACE FACES, HE LEARNED THE MYTHICAL "SECRET SAYINGS" OF THE STAFF. ONE FUDGE METEOR SHOWER AND A SMALL BELLYACHE LATER, HE WAS A WHIZ AT READING NOTES ON THE STAFF, AND READY FOR HIS NEXT MUSICAL DESTINATION.

"On the musician's journey, learning tricks (and even shortcuts) can help us find our way around in the beginning. We know we are on our way when the use of tricks and tactics is replaced by knowledge and skill."

– The Meridee Winters Guidebook to the Musical Universe

TELESCOPIC TIPS:

Earthling music teachers disagree as to whether mnemonic devices (quick memorable sayings to help recall information) are a helpful trick for learning your way around the staff or an unnecessary crutch. One thing earthling music teachers agree about is that you shouldn't use mnemonic devices forever. Don't get "hooked on mnemonics," but they are a fun and often useful tool.

See **"Ways to Play"** on page 3 for tips to make this chapter even more fun and impactful.

Space Face

MERIDEE WINTERS' MUSIC METHOD

Every Good Boy Deserves Fudge

MERIDEE WINTERS® MUSIC METHOD

Feeling bold? Skip ahead and try a challenge from the interval chapter!

DON'T DO IT

Star Log

Record your best times on the Star Log Score Sheets in the back. ➞

MERIDEE WINTERS' MUSIC METHOD

All Cows Eat Grass

MERIDEE WINTERS' MUSIC METHOD

Star Log

Record your best times on the Star
Log Score Sheets in the back. ➔

⭐⭐⭐⭐⭐

MERIDEE
WINTERS'
MUSIC METHOD

Good Birds Don't Fly Away

MERIDEE WINTERS' MUSIC METHOD

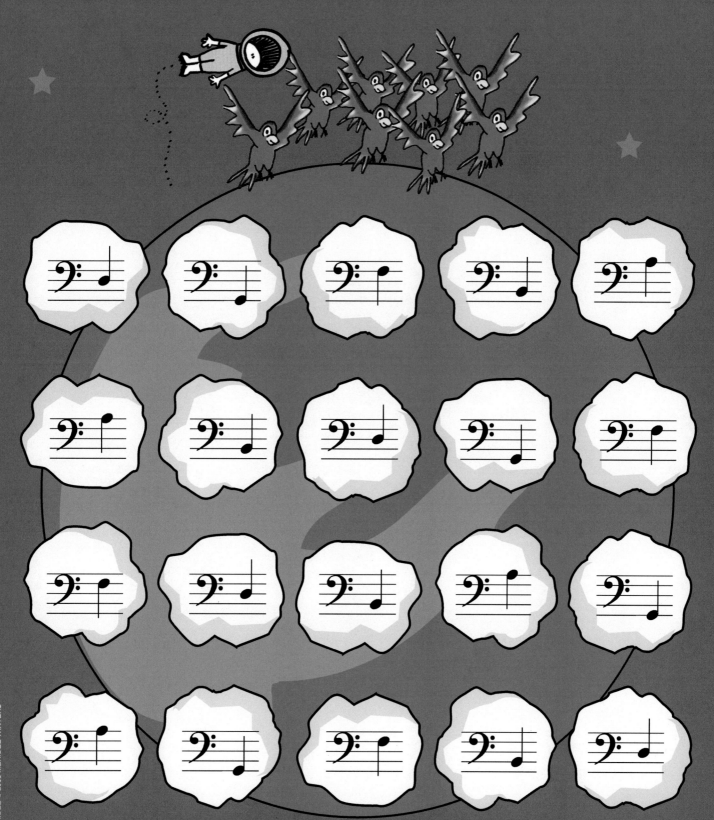

Star Log

Record your best times on the Star Log Score Sheets in the back. →

Creativity Zone

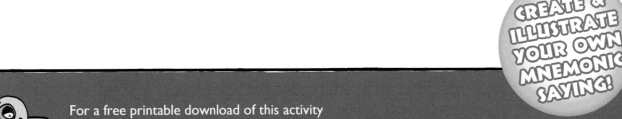

For a free printable download of this activity and other fun stuff, visit **mwfunstuff.com/nqp**

MAGICALLY MADE FOR YOU BY MERIDEE © 2008 MERIDEE WINTERS®

NORMAN'S NEXT ADVENTURE TOOK HIM TO A VARIETY OF ASTEROID BELTS, ALL IN DIFFERENT POSITIONS IN THE GALAXY. HE VISITED C POSITION, G POSITION AND MORE, WHILE MEETING ONE INTERESTING CREATURE AFTER ANOTHER. (SPACE SNAKES ARE PRETTY FRIENDLY, AS IT TURNS OUT.)

"He who plays slowly moves faster; she who works small learns big. Zoom in and master a small piece at a time. Zoom out when you are ready to take on more. The art of focusing reduces mistakes that actually slow us down."

— The Meridee Winters Guidebook to the Musical Universe

TELESCOPIC TIPS:

Learning on a piano keyboard is just like learning on a typing keyboard. It is most effective to drill and master a few keys at a time, and then add on other keys later.

Each "location" in this chapter focuses on a specific common hand position on the keyboard, with individual hands and hands together: middle C position, C position, G position and treble C. It is especially useful to use these drills to refresh note-reading skills before learning a song in the correlating hand position.

See "**Ways to Play**" on page 3 for fun spins to use when playing.

MERIDEE WINTERS' MUSIC METHOD

Dolphin Dipper

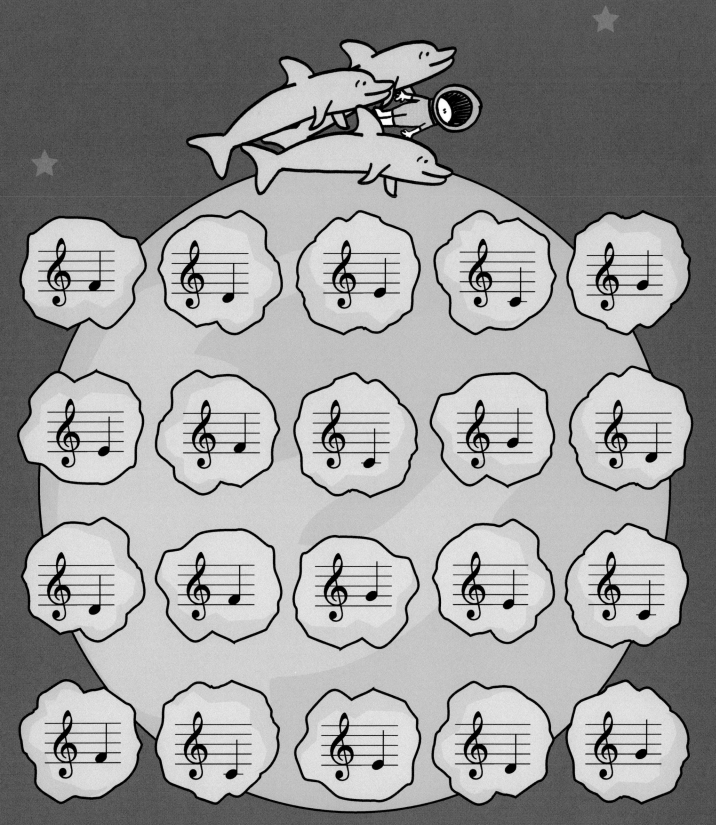

Star Log

Record your best times on the Star
Log Score Sheets in the back. ➡

Galactic Goldfish

Star Log

Record your best times on the Star Log Score Sheets in the back. ➡️

Octopus Orbit

Star Log

Record your best times on the Star Log Score Sheets in the back. →

MERIDEE WINTERS MUSIC METHOD

Star Log

Record your best times on the Star Log Score Sheets in the back. →

Jellyfish Jetstream

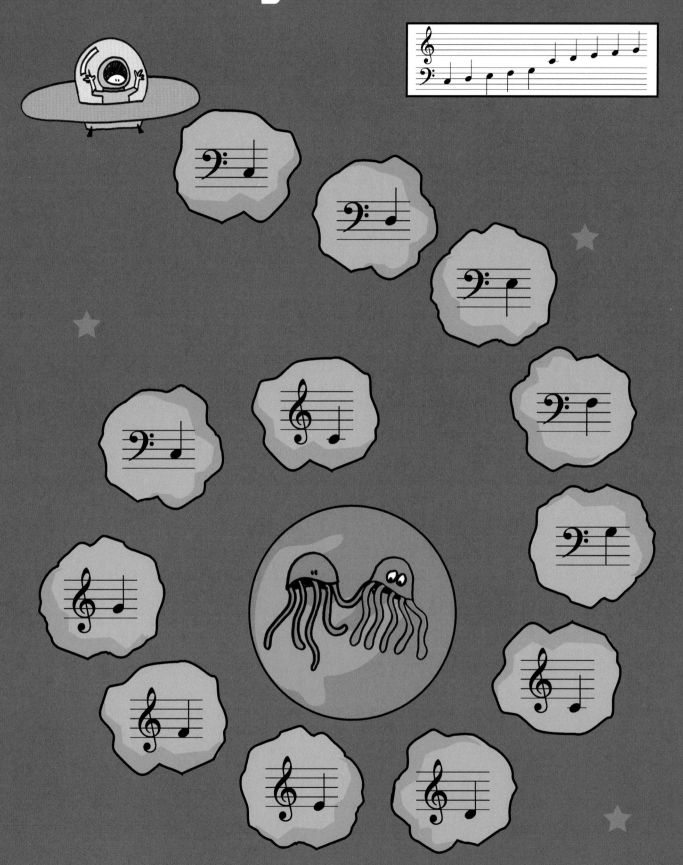

MERIDEE WINTERS' MUSIC METHOD

Star Log

Record your best times on the Star
Log Score Sheets in the back. ➞

Frog Fusion

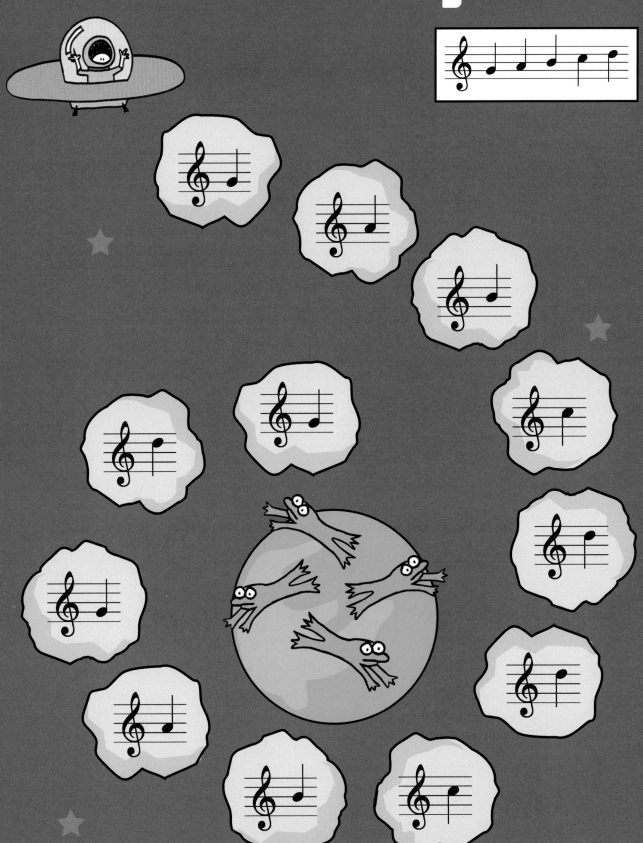

Star Log

Record your best times on the Star Log Score Sheets in the back. ➡

extra-tur-restrial

Feeling bold? Skip ahead and try a challenge from the interval chapter!

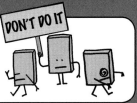

DON'T DO IT

Star Log

Record your best times on the Star Log Score Sheets in the back. ➡

Snake System

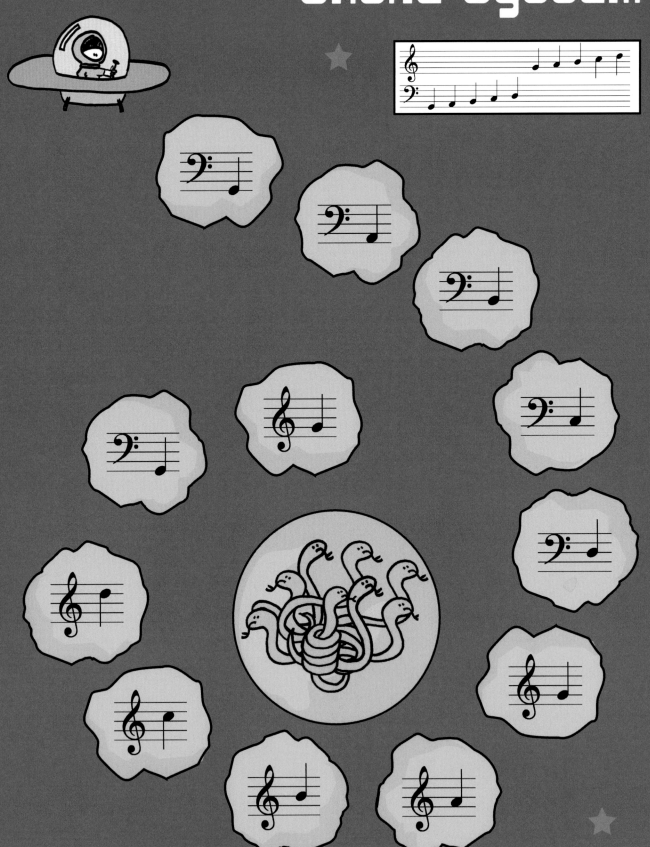

MERIDEE WINTERS' MUSIC METHOD

Star Log

Record your best times on the Star Log Score Sheets in the back. ➡

Various Aquarius

MERIDEE WINTERS' MUSIC METHOD

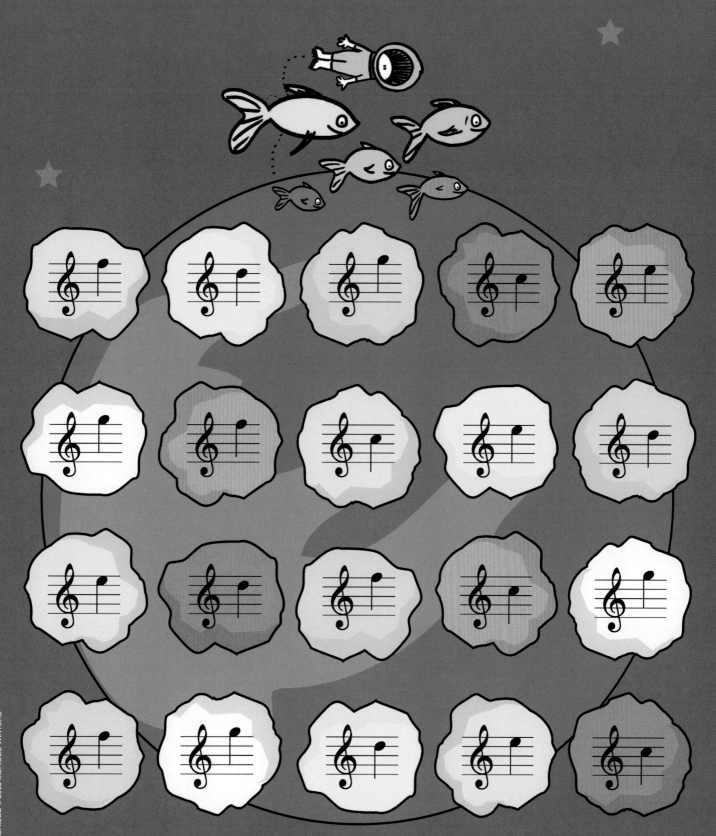

Star Log

Record your best times on the Star
Log Score Sheets in the back. →

Creativity Zone

For a free printable download of this activity and other fun stuff, visit **mwfunstuff.com/nqp**

MAGICALLY MADE FOR YOU BY MERIDEE © 2008 MERIDEE WINTERS®

MERIDEE WINTERS® MUSIC METHOD

WHEN HE WAS STILL IN MUSIC LESSONS ON PLANET BLAH, NORMAN DREADED READING LEDGER LINES – ALL MUSIC STUDENTS DID. BUT WHEN HE FOUND HIMSELF IN THE "DREADED" LEDGER LANDS OF SPACE, NORMAN FOUND THAT THEY WERE NOT DREADFUL AT ALL! HE WAS SURPRISED BY HOW WELL HE WAS ABLE TO NAVIGATE THEM BY FOCUSING ON JUST A FEW NOTES AT ONCE.

"Mastering a challenge is best achieved by shining your attention like a laser beam into the dark, difficult places. Spotlight a tiny section and practice it intentionally. Failure is assured if you take on too much, play it too fast, or try to ignore that the challenge exists."

– The Meridee Winters Guidebook to the Musical Universe

TELESCOPIC TIPS:

Ledger lines are often a stumbling block for beginning to intermediate musicians, but by isolating them and strengthening the skill, you can go from ledger-phobe to ledger-fan.

To learn more about isolating skills, finding flow and creating success, visit us at **merideewintersmusicmethod.com**

DREADED LEDGER LANDS

MERIDEE WINTERS' MUSIC METHOD

Free as a Bee

MERIDEE
WINTERS®
MUSIC METHOD

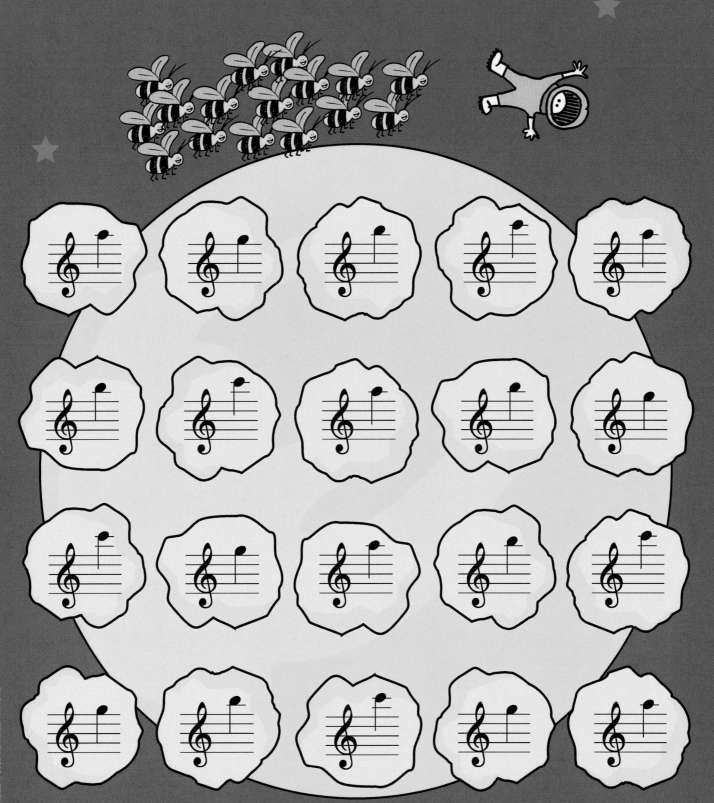

Star Log

Record your best times on the Star Log Score Sheets in the back. →

Ant-i Gravity

MERIDEE WINTERS® MUSIC METHOD

If you feel brave, skip ahead and try a challenge from the Grand Staff Grand Finale Chapter!

DON'T DO IT

Star Log

Record your best times on the Star Log Score Sheets in the back. →

Spider Spinners

Star Log

Record your best times on the Star Log Score Sheets in the back. ➡️

MERIDEE WINTERS' MUSIC METHOD

Creativity Zone

For a free printable download of this activity
and other fun stuff, visit **mwfunstuff.com/nqp**

CREATE
YOUR OWN
SPACE
SCENE!

MERIDEE
WINTERS'
MUSIC METHOD

NORMAN WAS READY TO BECOME AN EVEN BETTER INTERGALACTIC EXPLORER. ALL GREAT EXPLORERS ARE EXPERTS ON THE CONCEPT OF DISTANCE, SO NORMAN'S NEXT DESTINATION WAS A PLACE WHERE HE COULD LEARN AND MASTER INTERVALS (THE DISTANCE BETWEEN TWO NOTES). WITH PRACTICE, HE WAS ABLE TO IDENTIFY INTERVALS BY QUICKLY LOOKING AT THEM – A NAVIGATIONAL (AND MUSICAL) SUPERPOWER!

"Innovative composers combine notes into intervals to create songs that inspire others. Innovative music lessons combine materials in different ways to inspire learning. Both have structure, but also go beyond structure to create their own customized symphonies."

— The Meridee Winters Guidebook to the Musical Universe

TELESCOPIC TIPS:

Being able to quickly recognize different intervals will strengthen your overall sight reading skills. These exercises are a great companion to the interval chapters of Meridee's piano pattern and chord books. Check out these books for yourself, and master intervals, chords and more!

Interval Intermission
Harmonic Seconds Through Fifths

MERIDEE WINTERS MUSIC METHOD

Interval Intermission
Harmonic Seconds Through Fifths

Inter-stellar
Melodic Seconds Through Fifths

MERIDEE WINTERS® MUSIC METHOD

Inter-galactic
Harmonic Seconds Through Octaves

Inter-galactic
Harmonic Seconds Through Octaves

Inter-Planetary
Melodic Seconds Through Octaves

MERIDEE WINTERS' MUSIC METHOD

Inter-Planetary
Melodic Seconds Through Octaves

Creativity Zone

 For a free printable download of this activity and other fun stuff, visit **mwfunstuff.com/nqp**

CREATE YOUR OWN CLOUD SCENE!

MERIDEE WINTERS' MUSIC METHOD

ONE DAY, NORMAN SAW SOMETHING IN THE DISTANCE. THE BORING FACTORY! HOW COULD IT BE? AS HE APPROACHED, HE LEARNED THE TRUTH: THIS WASN'T THE FACTORY FROM PLANET BLAH AT ALL – THE UNIVERSE HAS BORING FORCES (AND BORING FACTORIES) EVERYWHERE. NORMAN FOUND HIMSELF DRAWN INTO ITS GRAVITATIONAL PULL, AND IT WOULD TAKE ALL HIS NEW SKILLS, AND ALL OF HIS CREATIVITY, TO ESCAPE.

IT WAS A TRUE TEST THAT WOULD SPAN THE ENTIRE STAFF. THE GRAND STAFF SHOWDOWN BEGAN.

 "Never lose touch with the creativity within. Those caught by the forces of boredom will often grow comfortable there. Rather than focusing your energy on why they should change, focus your energy on what you can create. Do not disturb the forces of boredom, and don't let them disturb you."

– The Meridee Winters Guidebook to the Musical Universe

TELESCOPIC TIPS:

In this chapter, you will prepare for the Grand Staff Grand Finale by practicing and polishing all of the notes on each staff. Many students are intimidated as they start playing songs that span the grand staff. By making it a game, these activities can work the skills in a less stressful (and more fun) way.

Boring Factory

MERIDEE WINTERS' MUSIC METHOD

Really Boring Factory

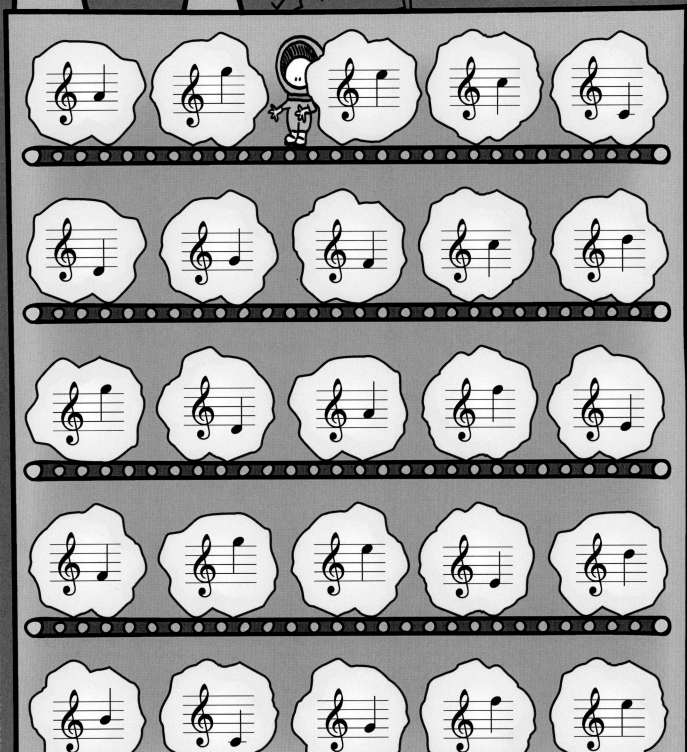

MERIDEE
WINTERS®
MUSIC METHOD

Super Boring Factory

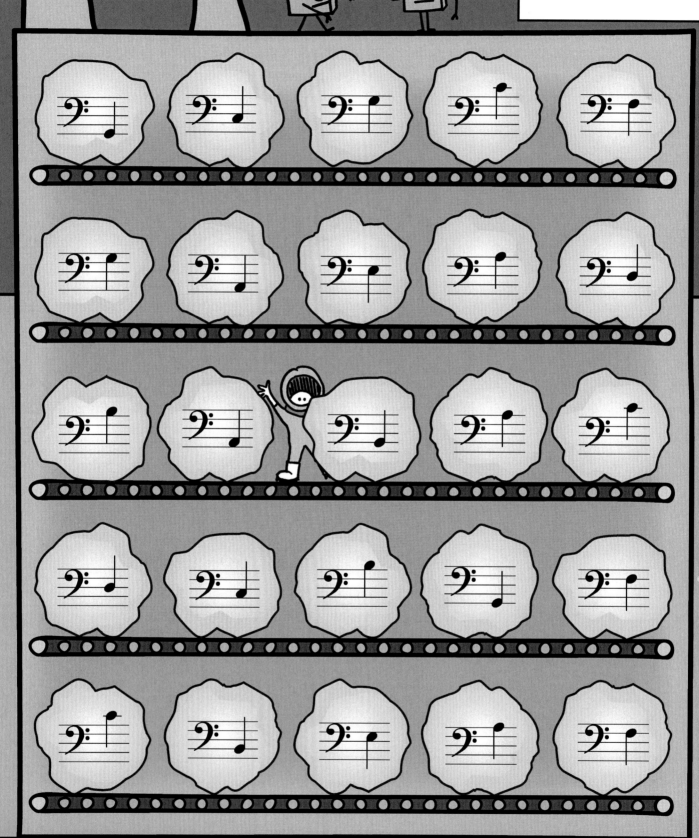

MERIDEE WINTERS® MUSIC METHOD

Extra Boring Factory

MERIDEE WINTERS® MUSIC METHOD

Amazingly Boring Factory

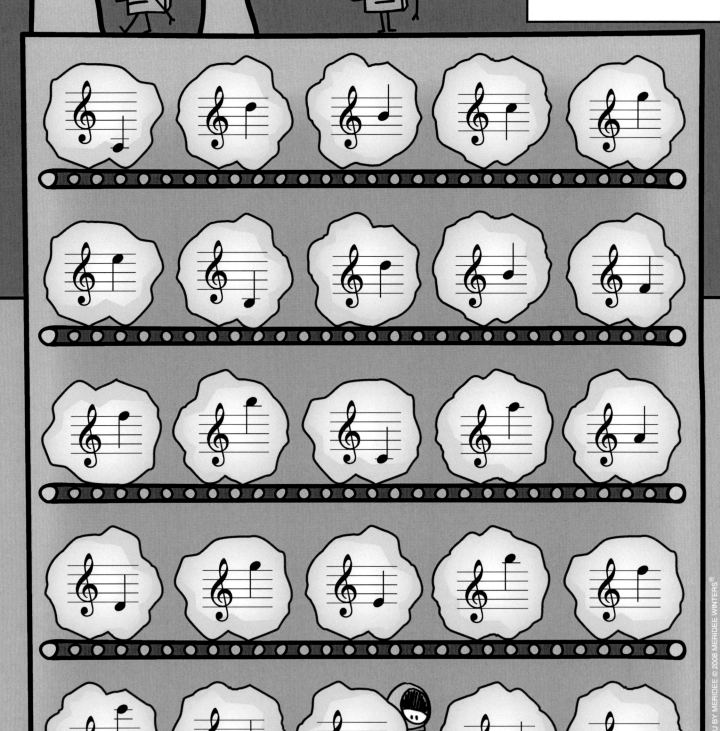

MERIDEE WINTERS® MUSIC METHOD

Extraordinarily Boring Factory

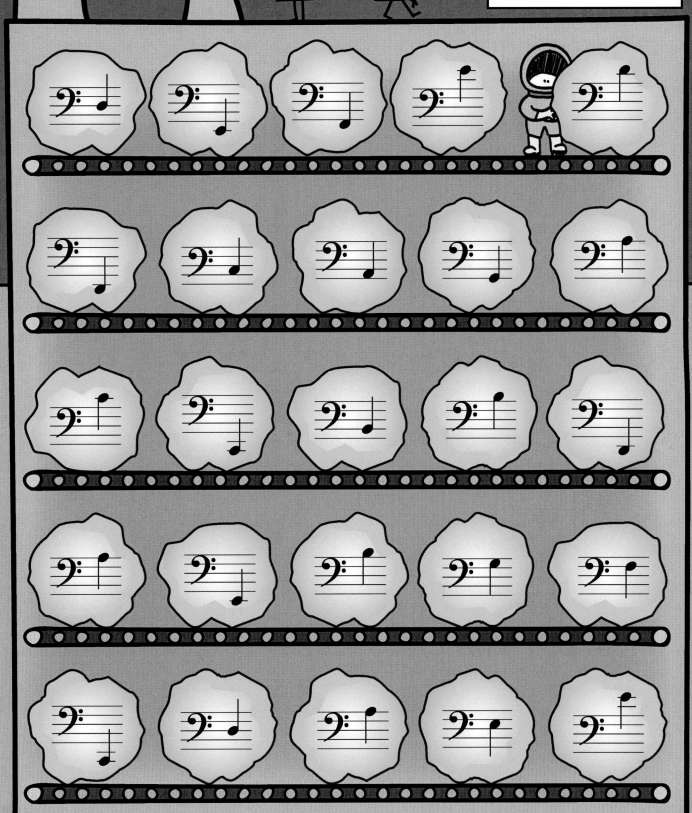

MERIDEE WINTERS' MUSIC METHOD

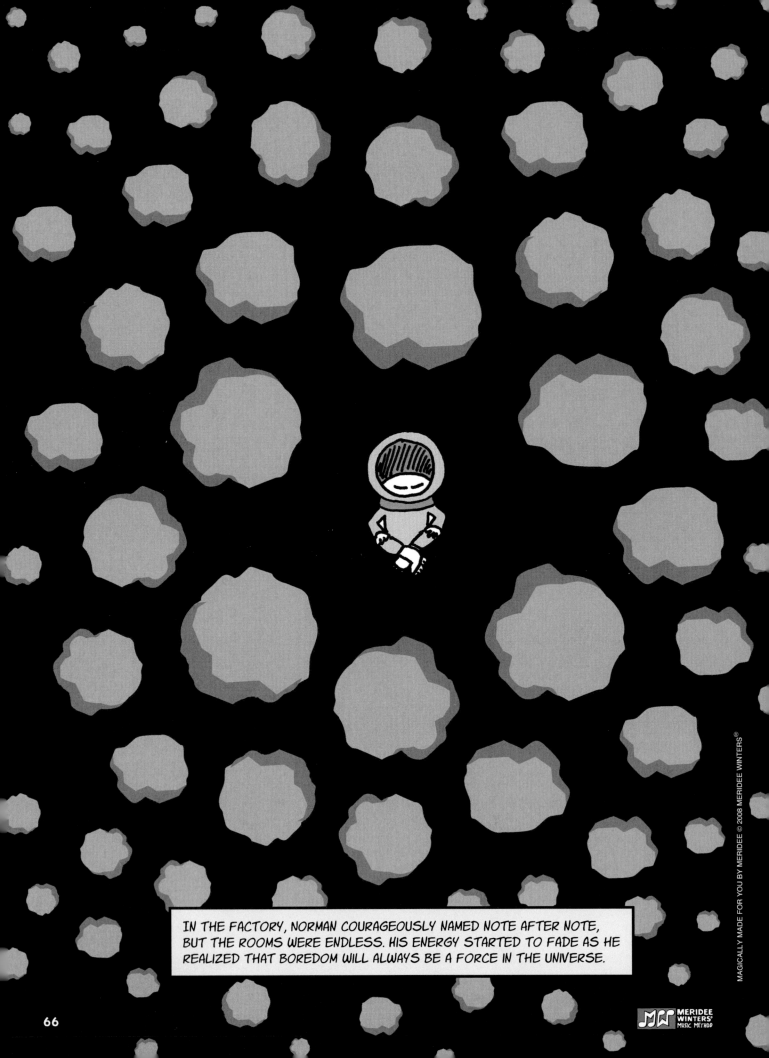

IN THE FACTORY, NORMAN COURAGEOUSLY NAMED NOTE AFTER NOTE, BUT THE ROOMS WERE ENDLESS. HIS ENERGY STARTED TO FADE AS HE REALIZED THAT BOREDOM WILL ALWAYS BE A FORCE IN THE UNIVERSE.

MERIDEE WINTERS' MUSIC METHOD

FINALLY, WHEN HIS ENERGY WAS NEARLY GONE, NORMAN CHANGED HIS APPROACH. HE FOCUSED ON HIS OWN CREATIVE POWER. WITH A BANG, THE BORING FACTORY WAS TRANSFORMED! IN ITS PLACE WAS A NEW WORLD OF CREATIVITY, WHERE MUSIC AND IMAGINATION THRIVED!

"One day, after studying all the pieces of the puzzle, you will get to put it all together and see the big picture of what you've learned."

*— The Meridee Winters Guidebook
to the Musical Universe*

TELESCOPIC TIPS:

After zooming in and isolating many different sight reading skills, you are ready to put them together and integrate them into the grand staff. The grand staff includes both the treble and bass clef, and reading both at the same time will be your biggest challenge yet. Apply your skills from the ledger line, mnemonic and other chapters to complete these pages. If you get stuck, try isolating the skills again by visiting an earlier chapter, and then returning to this chapter to integrate the skills back into these more challenging activities.

Big Bang

A New World

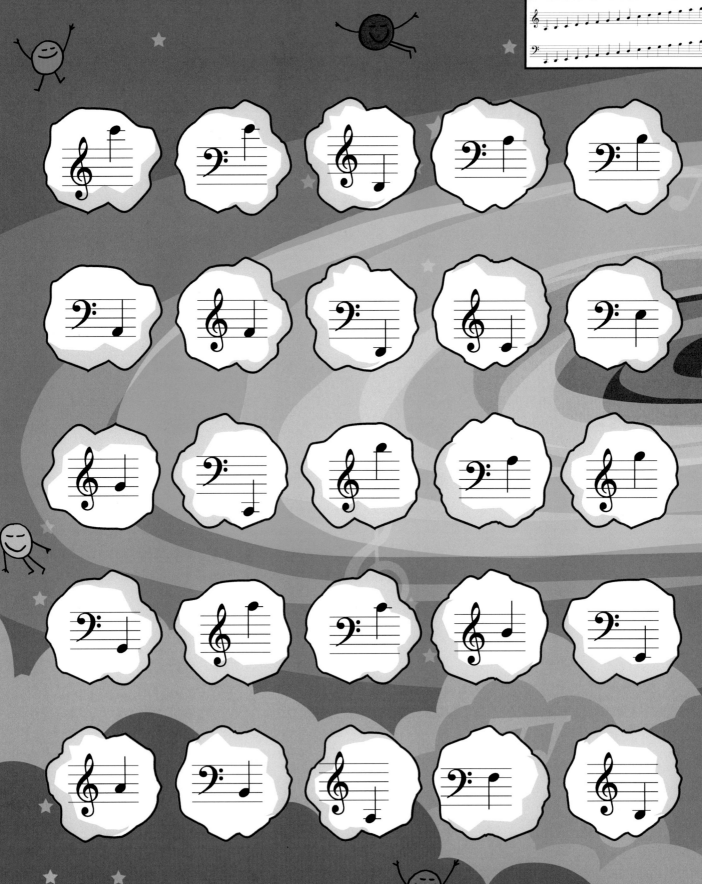

MERIDEE WINTERS' MUSIC METHOD

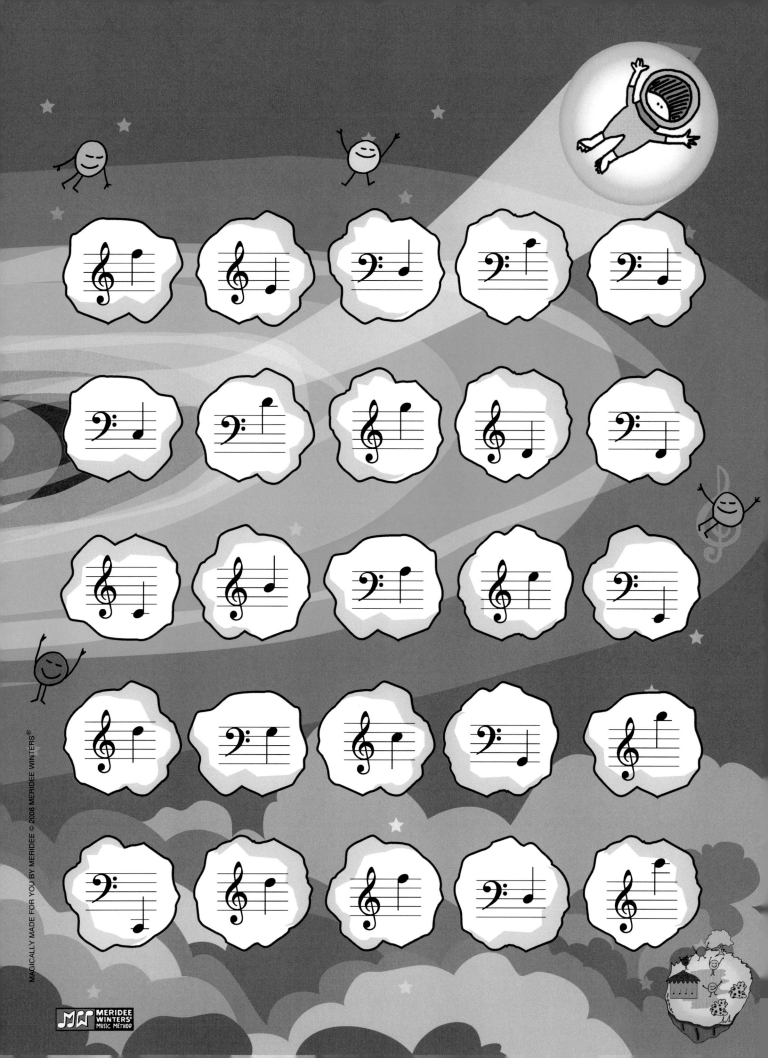

SORRY BORING BOOK ZOMBIES! WE CHOOSE CREATIVITY!
DON'T LISTEN TO HER!
For more creative stuff, visit us at mwfunstuff.com/nqp

NOW IT IS YOUR TURN TO CREATE NEW WORLDS, NEW STORIES AND YOUR OWN ADVENTURES.

DID YOU KNOW YOU ARE PART OF THE CREATIVE UNIVERSE, TOO? THE MUSICAL UNIVERSE IS ALWAYS CHANGING AND GROWING, SO ADD TO IT NOW WITH YOUR OWN MUSICAL CREATIONS.

FOR MORE COPIES OF THESE CREATIVE TEMPLATES OR TO SHARE YOUR IDEAS, VISIT MWFUNSTUFF.COM/NQP

"Sometimes we need the safety of lines and boundaries to start filling in our own ideas. Then, when we're ready, we can break free and boundlessly create."

— The Meridee Winters Guidebook to the Musical Universe

TELESCOPIC TIPS:

Every part of the Meridee Winters Music Method has a "create your own" option, and everything we do is an invitation to create and empower. Use these game forms, and our many others available, to customize games to specific skill sets, lessons, or even holidays and hobbies. Create your own music games on and outside the forms to take charge of your own learning.

MERIDEE WINTERS' MUSIC METHOD

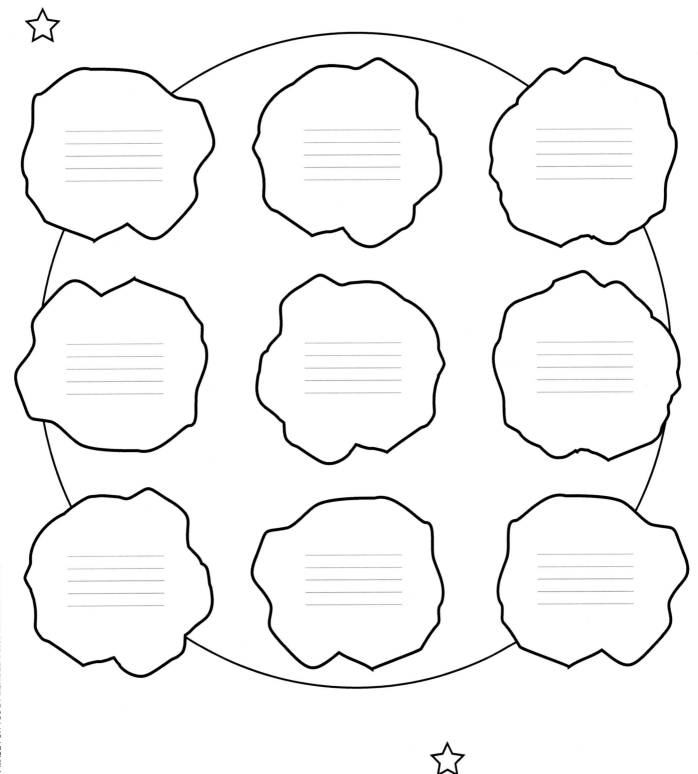

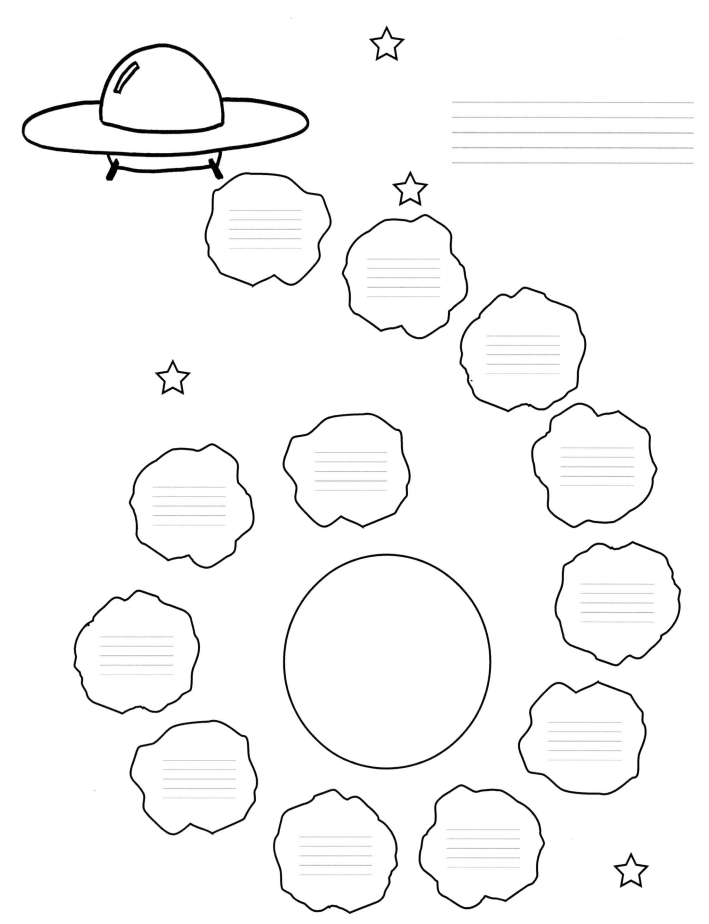

 MERIDEE WINTERS' MUSIC METHOD

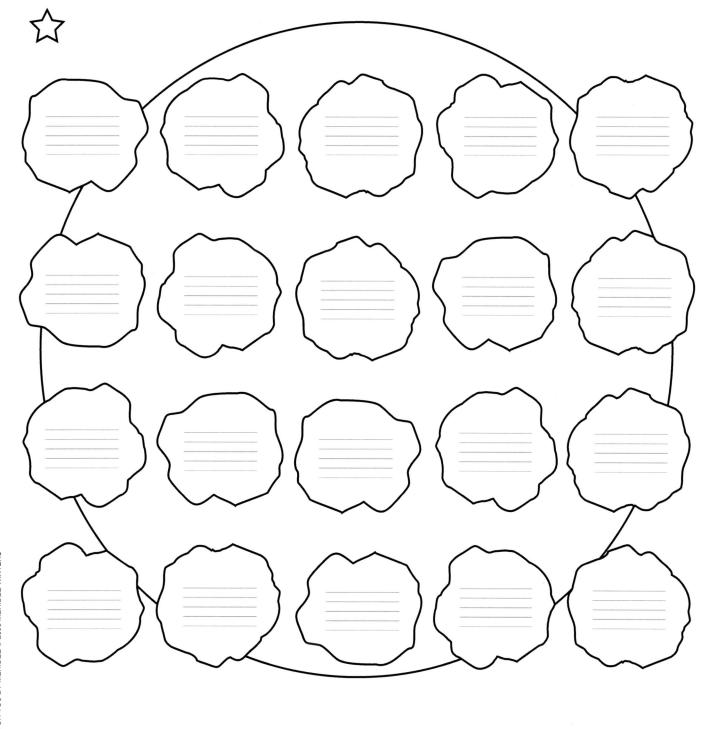

TITLE _____

YOU NOW KNOW THE ENDING OF NORMAN'S STORY. WHAT'S YOUR STORY? WHAT ARE THE BORING FORCES IN YOUR LIFE, AND HOW DO YOU OVERCOME THEM TO CREATE?

Psst! Turn to page 89 to see another comic, and to learn about the Meridee Winters School of Music's history!

AWARD

THE
ORB
OF
NOTE-ABILITY

IS HEREBY GIVEN TO

_____

FOR

_____

_____

_____

The adventure has just begun!

To download copies of this (or other fun stuff)
go to **mwfunstuff.com/nqp**

MERIDEE WINTERS' MUSIC METHOD

Star Log

★ ★ ★ ★ ★

Page/Game	Date/Time				
SPACE FACE	Date: MAR. 2ND Time: 1M 12s	Date: MAR. 9TH Time: 55s	Date: MAR. 23RD Time: 49s	Date: Time:	Date: Time:
	Date: Time:	Date: Time:	Date: Time:	Date: Time:	Date: Time:
	Date: Time:	Date: Time:	Date: Time:	Date: Time:	Date: Time:
	Date: Time:	Date: Time:	Date: Time:	Date: Time:	Date: Time:
	Date: Time:	Date: Time:	Date: Time:	Date: Time:	Date: Time:
	Date: Time:	Date: Time:	Date: Time:	Date: Time:	Date: Time:
	Date: Time:	Date: Time:	Date: Time:	Date: Time:	Date: Time:
	Date: Time:	Date: Time:	Date: Time:	Date: Time:	Date: Time:
	Date: Time:	Date: Time:	Date: Time:	Date: Time:	Date: Time:
	Date: Time:	Date: Time:	Date: Time:	Date: Time:	Date: Time:
	Date: Time:	Date: Time:	Date: Time:	Date: Time:	Date: Time:
	Date: Time:	Date: Time:	Date: Time:	Date: Time:	Date: Time:

For a free printable download of this activity
and other fun stuff, visit **mwfunstuff.com/nqp**

Page/Game	Date/Time				
	Date: Time:	Date: Time:	Date: Time:	Date: Time:	Date: Time:
	Date: Time:	Date: Time:	Date: Time:	Date: Time:	Date: Time:
	Date: Time:	Date: Time:	Date: Time:	Date: Time:	Date: Time:
	Date: Time:	Date: Time:	Date: Time:	Date: Time:	Date: Time:
	Date: Time:	Date: Time:	Date: Time:	Date: Time:	Date: Time:
	Date: Time:	Date: Time:	Date: Time:	Date: Time:	Date: Time:
	Date: Time:	Date: Time:	Date: Time:	Date: Time:	Date: Time:
	Date: Time:	Date: Time:	Date: Time:	Date: Time:	Date: Time:
	Date: Time:	Date: Time:	Date: Time:	Date: Time:	Date: Time:
	Date: Time:	Date: Time:	Date: Time:	Date: Time:	Date: Time:
	Date: Time:	Date: Time:	Date: Time:	Date: Time:	Date: Time:
	Date: Time:	Date: Time:	Date: Time:	Date: Time:	Date: Time:
	Date: Time:	Date: Time:	Date: Time:	Date: Time:	Date: Time:

Notes

MAGICALLY MADE FOR YOU BY MERIDEE © 2008 MERIDEE WINTERS®

Back on the Grand Staff, Norman's explosion of creativity was so powerful that many notes were freed from the staff. They danced in excitement – or at least, they tried to. It quickly became clear that there was something missing: rhythm.

Just as they were deliberating where to find this much-needed rhythm, Meridee stopped by in her imagination bubble and told them about Rhythm Village – a series of tropical islands a few solar systems away in her Game Galaxy.

A few poorly-timed beats later, they were on their way to their next adventure in Rhythm Village. (And you can join them!)

LEMON VILLAGE

SUPERCHARGE Your Progress
with The Meridee Winters
Homework Book & Practice Tracker!

GLOSSARY

USE THIS SECTION TO RECORD NEW TERMS AND CONCEPTS AS YOU LEARN THEM.

EACH BOX HAS 5 LINES... YOU CAN USE IT LIKE NOTEBOOK PAPER OR A STAFF!

Fermata: A fermata is a symbol written over a note that instructs you to hold it out for longer than written.

THE CIRCLE OF FIFTHS

MY GREATEST HITS...

AS YOU MASTER A SONG, WRITE IT DOWN HERE. YOU'LL HAVE A GO-TO LIST (CALLED A REPERTOIRE) OF SONGS YOU CAN PLAY FOR FRIENDS, FAMILY AND FUN.

GOALS AND DREAMS

WHAT I WANT TO LEARN:

INSPIRATION, DOODLES AND FAVORITE SONGS

MY TEACHER'S GOALS:

FILL OUT A MINI VERSION OF YOUR GREATEST HITS AND GOALS AND DREAMS NOW!

Magically made for you by Meridee © 2018 Meridee Winters®

Magically made for you by Meridee © 2018 Meridee Winters®

2

Available in a variety of instruments and covers. Get results and have fun! These books include assignment pages, goal-setting tools, theory tools, practice trackers and more!

the **MERIDEE WINTERS** school of music story

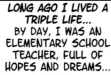

LONG AGO I LIVED A TRIPLE LIFE... BY DAY, I WAS AN ELEMENTARY SCHOOL TEACHER, FULL OF HOPES AND DREAMS...

Test today

HI! I'M MERIDEE!

BY AFTERNOON, I LED A SUCCESSFUL KARATE SCHOOL...

AND AT NIGHT, I ROCKED OUT WITH MY BAND!

AS MUCH AS I LOVED MY TRIPLE LIFE, SOMETHING WAS MISSING. AT SCHOOL, THE PRINCIPAL FORCED ME TO FOLLOW THE SAME BORING CURRICULUM EVERY YEAR, AND IN MY BAND, WE ONLY PLAYED COVER SONGS.

MY LIFE NEEDED... **CREATIVITY!**

SO I QUIT MY JOB, SOLD THE KARATE SCHOOL, LEFT THE BAND AND STARTED OUT ON A JOURNEY.

....TRAVELING THE WORLD TO LEARN ABOUT CREATIVITY AND SONGWRITING.

I STUDIED WITH WISE OLD SORCERERS, FOUGHT FIRE-BREATHING DRAGONS, AND HONED MY MAGICAL MUSICAL SKILLS.

(OK... MAYBE THERE WEREN'T DRAGONS, BUT THERE WERE CRAZY OLD PROFESSORS AND STUCK UP ROCK STARS.)

Magical Music Secrets

WITH MY NEWFOUND WISDOM, I DECIDED TO START A SCHOOL THAT COULD TEACH OTHERS ABOUT THE WONDERS OF CREATIVITY.

mw music

NOW ALL OF THESE THINGS ARE A PART OF **YOUR MUSIC** LESSONS!

I CREATED BOOKS...

...AND GAMES...

PIANO PATTERNS

PIANO HOMEWORK JOURNAL

RHYTHM VILLAGE

GUITAR HOMEWORK JOURNAL

CHORD CRASH COURSE

IN TIME, WORD SPREAD ABOUT THESE MAGICAL MUSIC LESSONS, AND THE SCHOOL BEGAN TO GROW.

...AND TRAINED THE BEST, MOST MAGICAL TEACHERS IN THE LAND!

WHAT SECRETS WILL YOU DISCOVER?

Illustrated by Rick Menard - www.rickmenard.com

Created by a former school teacher, the Meridee Winters Music Method was created as a solution to a problem: that lesson and exercise books teach at the "rote and recall" level, with little room for creativity.

There is also a need for great music materials for learners of all styles, including gifted learners, young learners, students that fall on the autism spectrum, those with dyslexia and more. The Meridee Winters Music Method tackles all of these complex needs with her playful, progress-boosting books and activities.

Love this journal? Want to play your favorite songs or write your own? Check out Chord Crash Course!

Meridee's "Chord Crash Course" provides piano students of all levels with essential musical skills, great results and a strong foundation for their own creativity.

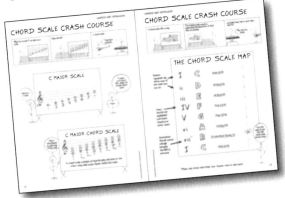

Sound great from the very first pages — whether you read music or not. Learn about intervals, chords and arpeggios, chord progressions, transposition, and more in this fun, trailblazing book.

WANT MORE CREATIVITY, MORE MUSIC, AND MORE MERIDEE?

Visit **merideewintersmusicmethod.com** for more great materials, special deals and articles on learning and teaching music!

MERIDEE WINTERS' MUSIC METHOD

Made in the USA
Middletown, DE
23 November 2018